DREWSTEIGNTON

A PORTRAIT OF A DARTMOOR PARISH AND ITS PEOPLE

DREWSTEIGNTON

A PORTRAIT OF A DARTMOOR PARISH AND ITS PEOPLE

JOHN CURNO

HALSGROVE

First published in Great Britain in 2001

Copyright © John Curno

British Library Cataloguing-in-Publication Data
A CIP record for this title is available from the British Library

ISBN 1 84114 135 6

HALSGROVE
Publishing, Media and Distribution

Halsgrove House
Lower Moor Way
Tiverton, Devon EX16 6SS
Tel: 01884 243242
Fax: 01884 243325
email sales@halsgrove.com
website www.halsgrove.com

Printed and bound in Great Britain by Bookcraft Ltd, Midsomer Norton

The book is dedicated to my wife Hilary

In memory of John Lally of York and Ron Catling of York

*With thanks to Barry Grantham of Lincoln for saving my life,
and thanks to Paul Greener and all the people who gave me information*

Drewsteignton from the church tower

Foreword

By Tom Ang

Few things now, if ever, are as they seem. If truth never resides on the surface, there's no guarantee, either, that it will be found under the surface. With their gentleness, loving touch and humour – acidulous at times – these images by John Curno are clearly not those of a passer-by, of an uninvolved photographer on a documentary day-job. Beware, then, the idyll implicit in the well-kept fields and the neat hedgerows. And the trees in the mist and clothes just-so rustic and not quite of their own time, engagingly give us timelessness – yet we really know how fragile it all is. For the idyll of the countryside is riddled with uncertainty about the future, tainted with the lingering odours of funeral pyres for innocent beasts, corrupted by the poor stewardship of a Government as distant as it is ignorant.

And so too, the images themselves: made in black and white, looking for all the world as if they were written with technology 150 years old. But they were taken with a digital camera whose workings are so modern few really understand what is going on inside the camera. Suffice that it works. A heavy parallel emerges then, between the countryside that is pleasant to visit, easy to forget so long as it works and photography that is fun, taken for granted until it fails. Neither is as it seems. We can enjoy the warmth of John Curno's images of his fellow villagers, we can enjoy the craft in his imagery. It is ours to dig deeper, to use both to care more.

Tom Ang

Author and Course Leader, Department of Hypermedia,
Photographic Arts and Sciences. University of Westminster, Harrow

John Curno, photographer. Taken by my daughter Rachel

Introduction

The idealistic image some people have of the countryside is often at odds with the reality of the present day.

I wanted to show the parish of Drewsteignton, the village, farms and surrounding area in the 21st century. My aim was also to record what the villagers and farmers looked like today amid the changes which increasingly affect rural areas. At present Drewsteignton is a parish largely unaffected by the rural revolution, its people very much seeing themselves as a community, with everyone making it a good place to live. The general store and post office, the church, the B & Bs and of course the pub make for a typical English village. People of all ages are included among my work, the young and not so young, and not forgetting the V.I.P.s (Very Important Pets).

Technology means increasing numbers of people work from home, using computers, working in the arts, travel and architecture, teachers of music and basketry. Many of these people have chosen a rural lifestyle over the bustle of urban life, only commuting when necessary. My photography reflects the impact of these new occupations along with the more traditional skills, while my photo essay on Blackaller Quarry and the men who worked there is an indication of how suddenly things that once seemed so permanent come to a close.

I have also included some landscape scenes and significant locations, from the prehistoric sites at Prestonbury and Cranbrook, and the enduring presence of Spinster's Rock, along with scenes familiar to the present-day.

There is no order of importance in these photographs, just some of the people and places that make up the parish as I see it. The fact that the images were taken over a short space of time (from Autumn 1999 to Spring 2001) is important for it shows the rapidity of change. Some of the people I have photographed are no longer among us, and in time all the scenes I have taken will fade from memory.

I was born in Plymouth, the youngest of ten children, in 1949. I became interested in photography in the late 1950s, but did not get a decent camera until the late 1960s (my first SLR was a Miranda Sensorex) and I joined the Pounds House Camera Club in Plymouth. I was mainly interested in the American photographers through reading magazines such as *Time*, *Life* etc., and found immediate empathy with the photography of Walker Evans, Wynn Bullock, Edward Weston, Minor White, along with some of the British photographers, including Frederick Evans.

I married in 1977 and we moved to York, where I discovered a real photographic gallery – Impressions – and a great group of friends also interested in photography. I think you have to be inspired to inspire and this gallery certainly set the spark off in me. I bought a Mamiya Press 6 x 9cm camera and later an MPP 5 x 4 inch and set off into the woods, the beach and on to the rooftops. By 1982 I had my own exhibition at Impressions Gallery, and travelled to many interesting destinations. I discovered and met some great British photographers including Martin Parr, Chris Killip, John Davies and John Blakemore. I became a professional photographer in 1985.

When we returned to Devon in 1993 we moved to Drewsteignton, but I did not re-establish the photographic business. I later sold most of my equipment and just took family photos. I became interested in digital photography in 1998 and began experimenting with the new medium, beginning my first serious work photographing my own parish of Drewsteignton, using a Nikon Coolpix 950 digital camera.

During the last year I have discovered that I live only a few miles from the photographer, Chris Chapman, whose work I have come to greatly admire. I regret that I did not know of or meet the late James Ravilious.

I hope that you enjoy these images of Drewsteignton parish. I thank everyone for their help and encouragement.

I would also like to thank everyone at Halsgrove for their work on this book, to Simon Butler, Karen, Denise, Lorna and all the others, thank you.

John Curno
June 2001

Some Parish Memories

An interview with Henry Scott – *June 2001*

Born at Bowden Farm, Drewsteignton in 1924, the youngest of three sons, Henry left school at 14, but during school days there was always plenty of work helping his father, Fred, and his grandfather on the farm. From the age of six or seven he would milk two or three cows before running to school.

His grandfather, Alfred Mudge, went to Bowden Farm in 1919, at the age of sixty, after being landlord of the Drewe Arms in Drewsteignton. His mother used to make butter which she took for sale at Newton Market on Wednesdays along with a few eggs and perhaps a few rabbits or chickens. With the money made from them, she would buy the groceries for the week.

Of course we had no electricity, no water rates, no telephone; the beauty of it used to be five gallons of oil from the oil man about once a month, that provided the lanterns and the old lamp on the kitchen table and that was the majority of the outlay. Grandmother made the bread; there was always a sack of flour in the dairy.

We used horse power; we always bred our own horses. You went out in the fields and caught a colt, mate[d] him, and you was on again. We would buy in wild colts too for about £30 and break them, and sell a good working horse for
about £60. *To pay the rent, we often used to sell a pair of horses in the spring of the year. For the Michaelmas rent, very often we had lambs, sheep and cattle that was gone out, and we always grew quite a bit of wheat as well, so there was the corn product.*

Bowden Farm was 200 acres and we were tenanted there. But over the years, as we prospered a little, we were able to start my brother off on a farm at Whiddon Down and we were able to buy various lots around here. We also bought some marshes at Exminster for summer grazing. We could expand in those days, but now you have to be very, very cautious.

In the thirties trade was very bad and a lot of farmers went bankrupt. There were three of them in the parish of Drewsteignton. No fault of their own, there was nowhere to borrow money. Banks wouldn't lend money. And those that had borrowed money after the Great War, when the Wall Street Crash was, the banks called in the money and, well of course, the farmers had to sell up and their farms were repossessed so there was no hope of them continuing.

When the war came prices shot up. All the land had to be ploughed and go in full production. Wages began to creep

Henry Scott and Will,
Brisdrew House

up gradually. In the thirties all a man had was 32s.6d and the stamp was 8d, which sometimes the farmer paid. Some poor chaps had to allow about 3s. a week for the rent of their house which was pretty drastic, especially if they had half a dozen children round the table. But as the war came on, the prices escalated and the countryside really got turned upside down. All the old ley fields, that is those bits that had been pasture for years, had to be ploughed. With the old landlord-and-tenant agreement you could only plough a certain acreage of the land and then you couldn't get the best out of the farm. But once you ploughed the farm in wartime, and turned it upside down, we had bumper crops. Course it was virgin soil nearly, never been ploughed for a hundred year.

In 1942 we changed from horses to tractor. We sold a good pair of horses for 207 guineas and with the money bought an iron-wheeled, new Fordson Major tractor for £176 and a plough as well. That ploughed the land all through the war. Today a tractor costs £30 000 and a five-furrow plough £17 000, but they cannot warrant all that money, its about ten times too bloody dear. It's more than what the farms cost! And then there's the massive combine. For a time me and my brother used to run a combine between us, we had 100 acres of cereal to do. But when we found we had to pay so much for belts and things, we had to have the contractors in.

Then the milk lorry started travelling, well that was just before the war, and all the farmers in the locality used to milk their cows and send the milk off on the lorry every morning.

You had a cheque first week in every month, which was a solid income and it worked very, very well for many years. Until it fizzled out, I suppose, about twenty year ago.

After the war there was quite a lot of money about, and on the land that was farmed well, the farmers done well. There was a good demand for all your cattle, don't matter what you had. During the war the Ministry of Food had taken over the buying of all the fat-stock. We were paid a standard rate, which we knew we were going to get six months before, so we could plan well ahead.

At the moment we haven't even got a market at all. And with this foot and mouth there is such a backlog of cattle, we don't know where we stand. And with this cattle crisis that we have at the moment; when its 30 months it has to go in the bin rather than going in the food chain, its absolutely ridiculous.

Nowadays is not the time to branch out, not by a long way, I can't see any return coming. If my son don't go out to work all the time he can, with his round baler and his muck spreader, he couldn't afford to stay here. We've had no income since last November when we sold the suckled cows which is the thing we produce. There's no demand now, because there's no movement allowed at the moment for them, so we have to wait. We're hoping that by Christmas they will be around again. The same for the sheep. I breed some Suffolk rams. I've got twenty out here. I don't know what sales are going to be. I may be able to make private sales with a lot of argy bargy and Ministry of Ag. forms and *them going to a clean area, but at the moment things are very static.*

I wouldn't like to say what the future holds for us, because people are going out of farming right, left and centre. There's hardly a young farmer left on the farms at all. Mechanisation has taken over. The only thing that the young farmer can do is to borrow father's equipment and go out and earn some money, because father can't afford to pay them the full rate of wages in comparison with the lads that go off to town. So the outlook is pretty bleak.

I don't think there will be many young farmers left in this locality. The majority that I know under forty are not interested at all, they will sell out. Those over forty, in my opinion, with the overheads high, they are struggling. The worst part of it is for those with families. The husband works the farm and the wife goes out to work as well. And the kids, well, if there isn't a grandmother to look after them then who is to fetch them off the (school) bus? But if the mother doesn't work, there is no way that they can afford to carry on. Not like we did, the old ways with mother staying at home to assist father a bit and doing all the cooking and mending and everything with the kiddies. Now she can't afford to stay home at all, it's impossible.

It will be hard to sell the land. But if somebody likes the property, there are some people with a hell of a lot of money to invest but they're not from the South West. I think Roger and Lainy (Chudley) are about the only two that was reared in Drewsteignton and have stayed here and live in their own

house. It's a great shame to think it was a village with so many families that go back generations and now about 80 per cent have gone; there are only a handful left that went to the local school.

The first thing the Government could do is to be interested in agriculture. Instead of flogging all our prime meat abroad and buying in all the cheap rubbish. Production costs have to be met and if there is no profit, well, no one can afford to carry on. At the moment the pig industry is worse than any of the rest, it's shocking.

The supermarkets have taken over, they are very strong. They put a selection of goods on the counter and even if they are losing on one thing they make enough profit on the rest. Many years ago the grocer sold groceries and the butcher sold the meat and that was the only place you got them. There was always country butchers, there used to be four butchers at Chagford in my young days, they used to kill their own. There is only one there now and he has a chain of shops. In Drewsteignton, Charlie [Hill's] grandfather used to slaughter his sheep there and sometimes, the odd bullock. It served the locality; but now people travel further. A lot of people are talking about this organic but I can't see it coming because the price of it is going to rule it out. If it tastes the same as the rest, I don't see that people are going to pay about 20 or 30 per cent more than for the rest.

The main thing is that today a lot of the lambs are slaughtered at about 12 or 14 weeks; well that always was a luxury at Easter time. But now, as soon as they are up to weight they'm off the farm; its not matured and good meat has got to be matured. A bullock was never fit to kill until he was 2 to 2½ years old. A pig was never really matured to pork until he was about a year old or more; but now when they kill it at six months, you score your crackling but it won't crackle. Its like rubber unless you've got an older pig, and that is always the luxury on a roast joint, to have the crackling. But it is supply and demand, they will buy the pigs when they are six months old. The farmer's got the lorry coming every Monday morning and he's got to put so much on the lorry, and that's his income coming in. Cash flow, that's the term they use nowadays. Lately we've had all these markets abroad, but with foot and mouth and BSE the door's shut, and I don't know when its going to be open again. The French in particular are going to take some persuading. I've always maintained the British slaughterhouses are second to none, the floor is fit to eat off of and the chaps are always turned out immaculate.

It's true that on Dartmoor they make more money on tourism. Tourists are all right up to a point. You only need a very wet year and the tourists don't come. So what then? Twenty year ago they said be careful with the buildings, the land is treasured and there's no more of it been made. But now they can't get rid of it fast enough, building like hell on it, and there's a terrific lot lost through erosion every year. If we've got good land capable of producing quite a bit of our food, it's a damn shame to think it is not kept in production and doing the job it is meant for. There should never be

these fields set aside, just growing weed for a year. When the war was over and the standard of farming had been 100 per cent, you would hardly see a thistle or a dock, and the hedges was all trimmed and the machinery was fairly good. But now all the men are gone from the farms; in our village there used to be about twenty going out every day to work on the farms, now I don't think there's one. It's getting like ghost towns, apart from the visitors that come.

When I got to 65 I began to see that a big change was coming in farming. I said to the young chap coming into the neighbouring farm, 'I'm going out and you are coming in, but I think I've had the best of it.' You're killed with officialdom, you can hardly move without having to sign a form now; it's going to take a long time before it gets back to plain sailing again.

I've always run a Land Rover. The one I've got now, I've had for ten year. I don't want a BMW to drive about the roads. My Land Rover serves me well; I can go across to see the cattle, put a sheep in the back and chuck the dog in. If you made money the hard way you'm reluctant to lose it. I like a bit of shooting and I like hunting – I'm a countryman. I enjoy going to market and sighting the different types of cattle that different people sell. I like to keep a high standard of bullocks. What I've got now, we've been breeding for several years. When we go to the suckle calf sale and general product market I like ours to be the best; that has always been my aim, and my father before me, keep a high standard.

Budbrooke Farm, Crockernwell

George Gillard and Ben,
Budbrooke Farm, Crockernwell

Chris and Liz Grosnay with Sasha and Cher, Natton Hall Farm

Stephen Bowden, Harepath Farm

Bethany Bowden and Drew,
Harepath Farm

Fred Duddridge, market gardener and beef farmer, Veet View Farm

'Dominator', harvesting time

International TD6 Crawler at Greystone Farm

East Fingle Farm, during the foot and mouth restrictions, Spring 2001

Tim Cordy with Bethany and calf, East Fingle Farm

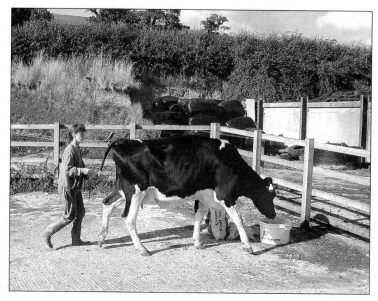

Tanya Cordy and Kylie,
East Fingle Farm

Steer called Big Boy, Greystone Farm

Cows at Higher Shilstone Farm

Graham Lock and Anne Loosemore, dairy farmers, Higher Fingle farm

Higher Fingle Farm

Greystone Farm, lambing time during the foot and mouth restrictions, Spring 2001

Richard Strong, Greystone Farm

Andrew Strong, Greystone Farm

Michael and John Strong (father), Greystone Farm

Bas and Jean Hollington with the Venton Flock

Sheep at Crockernwell

Sheepish indecision

Cross Farm

Dennis Hawke, farmer, Cross Farm

Preston Farm

Glyn, Ian and Benjamin Rowe with Herbie, Mill Farm, Whiddon Down

Martin, Kelly, Becky and Danielle Webber with Oxenacres Happy, Smiths Cross Farm

Charles Whelpton retired farmer, East Tordown Farm

Mollie Dunn, farm secretary

Harold Dunn, Dunn's Dairy

Catherine Dunn, Dunn's Dairy, Beacon View Farm

Roland Saffin, Fingle Farm

Neil Saffin, butcher, Fingle Farm

Tim Cox, Preston Barns

Martin Hutchings working at Preston Barns

Charlie Hill

Born in the parish, at Veet Mill in 1925, Charlie moved to Nethercott Farm in Spreyton when he was nine. On leaving school he farmed with his father, James. He and Jessie got married in 1952 and they moved to Barton Farm in Spreyton in 1965. In 1986 they sold up and moved into the old butchers' shop in Drewsteignton, which had been run by his uncle Sam.

Charlie and Jessica Hill with Coley

Sonny and Kath Martin

Sonny and Kath Martin

Sonny was born in the parish, at Harepath Farm in 1924, the youngest of eight children. His mother died when he was one year old and he went to live at Bowbeer Farm. He went to school in Drewsteignton and later to Crediton Grammar School. Sonny started work on the farm with his uncle Alf at the age of sixteen. He retired into the village of Drewsteignton when he was 62. Sonny likes his cricket.

Kath was born in Whitestone in 1930, but the family moved to Drewsteignton when she was 10. Her father Norman Courtney was a woodsman, working for the Ministry of Supply. Kath went to the village school for a year and then to Chagford. After school she started work at Drewston, then in 1953 she started working at Castle Drogo and stayed there until her retirement in 1999. At the age of twenty-five Kath married Les Gidley; he died in 1980. Kath married Sonny in 1996 and is enjoying her retirement.

Georgina Robinson

Born in 1919 Georgina lived in Chagford, married and moved to Drewsteignton in 1939. She was a cook at the Royal Hotel in Crockernwell and also worked at Puddicombe House. Finally she worked with Aunt Mabel in the Drewe Arms before retiring. Sadly she died early in 2001.

Georgina Robinson

Reg and Lucy Gidley

Reg Gidley

Born in Drewsteignton, at Church Gate in 1919. His father, Walter, was a timber merchant, getting wood from Dartmoor and taking it by horse and cart to Veet Sawmill. Reg went to the local school and left at the age of fourteen to start as an apprentice with Mr Partridge, the local builder and undertaker. He was in the Army during the war and went to France as an anti-aircraft gunner. After leaving the army he went back to work for Mr Partridge. He retired at the age of sixty-five.

Reg met his wife, Lucy, in Drewsteignton more than fifty years ago. She was born in India.

William Graham Morison

Born in Ireland in 1915, Graham moved to England as a child, and was educated at Oxford. He wanted to work in Africa, and applied to join the Colonial Service. He got a letter from Sarawak Offices (which was not a part of Colonial Services) so he went there instead to work in the treasury, and later on as an administrative officer.

During the Second World War he was a civilian internee (prisoner of war) of the Japanese for 3½ years, before being relieved by the Australians.

He returned to England and married. He was recalled to Sarawak in the late 1940s where he became District Officer of Affairs for the entire district around Kuching (the capital of Sarawak). Then he joined a new department – as a Registrar and Commissioner for Co-operative Development – until he retired in 1963. Sarawak is now part of Malaysia.

His parents had bought the Old Rectory in Drewsteignton and later he helped finance the building of the bungalow 'The Orchard'. When his parents died they left him the bungalow, where he has lived since the early 1970s.

W.G. Morison, retired District Officer of Affairs, Sarawak, Borneo

Jill Jory

Born in London. She was an officer in the WRNS during the war doing a lot of night duty, working on decoding the Enigma Code. She moved to Drewsteignton a few years ago.

Jill Jory, retired WRNS officer, Charisma Cottage

Pam Bridgeman

Born at Church Gate in Drewsteignton in 1941, she is the daughter of Georgina Robinson. She went to primary school in the village and then to Chagford Secondary School. She started work at 15 as a waitress at the Royal Hotel in Crockernwell and later worked at Wippells, academic and clerical tailors, making bishops' mitres. She married Clarence in 1963. In 1979 Pam went to work at Castle Drogo as a conservation cleaner, remaining there for the next 20 years.

Pam Bridgeman and Minty

James Clifton, actor, Silkhouse

James Clifton

Born in Lille, France, he moved to England at the age of four to live in the village of Chardstock in Devon. He went to the grammar school in Ilminster and then did a course in engineering at Shrewsbury College. His ambition was to go on to the stage and he got into RADA at the age of 24. After that he had various jobs until securing a contract with Rank. He appeared in a number of films for them including 'A Tale of Two Cities'. He also did stage and television work for the BBC and ITV, including working with Tony Hancock and appearing in one of the first soaps on the BBC called 'Our Miss Pepperton', which went out live twice a week.

Later his life took a new direction and he was in the rag trade for twenty years before retiring back to Devon, to Drewsteignton. He has lived here for the last twenty years, which he said has been one of the best times of his life. Currently a couple of James's dogs, his cow and his horse are being used in filming the second series of 'Down to Earth' for television. His lovely house and gardens have featured in a number of magazines.

Ernest Northway

Born in Chagford in 1909 at Middlecott Farm, Ernest moved to Drewsteignton in 1940. He worked for a local builder, Mr Partridge, as a carpenter and decorator. He was married to Marie Louise for twenty-five years; she passed away in 1997. Ernest also lost one of his best friends, Norman Webber, recently. He lives on his own in his lovely little house.

Ernest Northway

Fiona Taylor and Fluffy

Fiona Taylor

Born in Drewsteignton in 1988, she went to primary school in Chagford and is now at Okehampton College. Fiona has two sisters Lisa and Louise. She helps with the younger children at Sunday School and used to ring the bells at the church. Fiona enjoys horse riding and walking. She rides Harvey and goes out with her mother, Joy, who rides Zenna. The family has two dogs, two cats and a very noisy lovebird. They also had four guinea pigs which died recently.

She enjoys living in the country and is aware of the good work done by the National Trust. A disadvantage is that her school friends tend to live further apart. She said it would be difficult to live in a city with all the noise and fumes.

Elaine Chudley

Elaine was born in Drewsteignton in 1946, an only child. Both her parents worked at the Drewe Arms and Elaine helped with the washing up there when she was nine years old. She went to Drewsteignton Primary School and later to a boarding school in Okehampton, only coming home for holidays. When Elaine left school she went to work at an accountant's office in Exeter, using car sharing to get there and back. She has seen a lot of changes in the village and thinks that the opening of the A30 dual carriageway, Castle Drogo becoming a National Trust property, and the opening of moorland walks have helped to put Drewsteignton on the map and have kept the local post office and pub going.

Elaine married Roger in 1965 and they have two daughters, Deborah and Rachael, who have both moved away. Elaine relaxes now with hobbies like swimming, reading, writing, walking and gardening.

Roger and Elaine Chudley

Barbara Mayo and Luc, the Old Barn

Anne Powell, Church Cottage

Barry and Pam Starling, nurseryman and florist, The Chine

Beryl Scott with Eucalyptus, Brisdrew House

Bill and Audrey Keily with Curly, Adamswell

Catherine Martineau, Drewston House, on a sponsored ride for the Historic Churches Trust

Dorothy Drew and son Ken, builder and undertaker, The Bungalow, Venton

Edward and Marjorie Dine, The Old School Drewsteignton

Gordon Ching, retired saddler, Crockernwell

Graham and Brenda Lunt, Drascombe Barton

Irene Tippett, Heather Cottage

Jean Partridge and Pip. Jean is a retired nurse

Joan Gowing-Scopes and Tigger, Lady House

John Savage and Scruffpup, Wisedom Cottage

John Sherlock, Sarah Augbaya and Jacob

John Shiell, photographer and Jackie Abey, artist

Kam and BSA M21, Japonica Cottage

Karen Hudd, Heather Cottage

Lucinda Emanuel

Stephen Emanuel, architect, The Old Rectory

Louis and Eleanor Emanuel

Michele with Tina and Loopy

Mike and Linda Weever, Pippin Cottage

Mike and Sally Ives, Pixies Cottage, Sandgate

Miss Smith

Mrs Stevens, piano teacher

Nancy Giles and Smudge. Nancy is a retired post lady living at Knowle Cottage

Norman Webber, retired gardener

*Lynne Webber and Liam
with Buzz, Fly and Wiggy*

Paul and Daphne Greener with Hannah

Paul and Linda Bartlett with Rowan and Millie

Pete and Jennifer Mullins with Rory and Douglas

Rachel Curno

Pauline Rowe, Glebe Cottage

Ann Hall, Rose Cottage, Venton

Dr Michael Hall and Tappell, Rose Cottage, Venton

Arthur Westcott, retired country horticultural superintendent, Rose Cottage, Venton

Sarah, Sam, Hannah and Harry Strong with Lucy and puppies, Narracott Cottages

Clarence Bridgeman, gardener

Sue Marindin, Broadmoor Cottage

Tom and Rebecca Bates

*Tom Martineau, retired farmer
and clock repairer, Drewston House*

Tony Watkins (retired doctor). Judging Wine at the annual Drewsteignton show, 2000

Wayne and Diane Mudge with Alison and Samuel

Wilf and Matthew Merrtens and Rupert Curno

Keith and Dulcie Tipper, 1 Hillmorhayes

Colin and Janice Sparks, The Drewe Arms

*Clive and Maureen Gribble
with Penny, The Old Inn*

Post Office and Store. Ron and Penny Hill with Ken Wood

Old Post Office

Ford House

Michael Page, Ford House

Parford, stables

View from the church tower

Parford's outbuildings

Brick Barn, Narracott

The Old School

Hob House

Barn at Fingle Farm

Barn at Drewston

Ruin, Honeyford

Hamish, Honeyford Cottage door

Shed at Fingle Farm

Allotment, Drewsteignton

Tomatoes and cucumbers

The Old Rectory

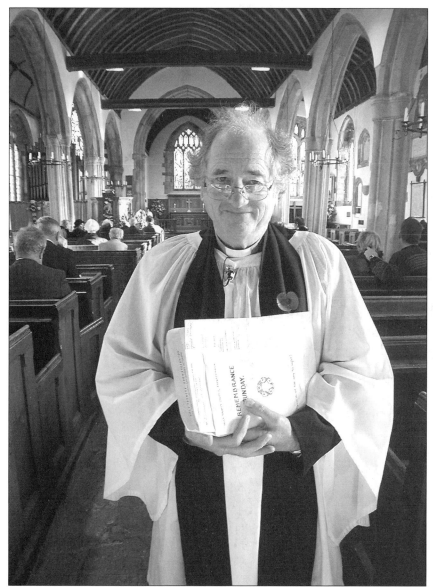

Church Choir

John Withers, Remembrance Day

Holy Trinity, Drewsteignton

Church End Cottages

Kenneth Floyd, church doorway

Castle Drogo gardens

Castle Drogo

Antique Fair, Castle Drogo

Caroline Brown, Honeyford Baskets

Scarlett Brown, Honeyford Cottage

George Watson, stonemason and builder

Dave Denford, blacksmith

Henry Alexander, walking sticks

Helen Chaloner, ARVON (creative writing course)

John Monk, hop planter

John Hooper, charcoal burner

John Loram. Manufacturer of agricultural buildings at West Fingle Farm

Rebecca Loram and Rosie, West Fingle Farm

Ken and June Ashburner, Mythic Gardens, Stone Farm

Mythic Gardens

*'The Listeners' by Jackie Abey and Jill Smallcombe,
Mythic Gardens*

Margaret Vile, church warden and Carol Price. Cream teas in Knowle Cottage

Mike Rowe, builder, working in the beer garden at the Drewe Arms

Ken Webber, forestry worker, Venton

Andy Phillips, milkman

Nigel Letheren

Nick Dixon, ornithologist

Oscar Emanuel with pole lathe

Paul Ching, saddler, Crockernwell

Paul Griggs, assistant butcher, Happy Hogs, Whiddon Down

Philip Evans, writer for R.H.S., West Netherton House

Paul Petrie-Ritchie, cabinet maker

Pete Taylor, painter and decorator

Peter Randall-Page, sculptor, Veet Mill

Kate Wilson, arts administration co-ordinator

Steve Pinn, hurdle maker

Sunday school with Ruth Merttens

Tim Hocking, Portakabin engineer, Venton

Toby Rubbra, Management Information Systems

Victoria Loram, teaches clarinet and piano, Hillmorhayes

John Gale, thatcher

Ashley Butler, arboriculturalist

John Bowers, dowsing at Spinsters Rock

Playing Fields, Sunday morning looking toward Cranbrook Castle

Locals gritting the roads

Riders. Joy Walker and Jennifer Grey

Robert Powlesand and Henry Scott, rough shooting

Trout fishing, River Teign

Crossroads at Greystone Cross

Fallen branch

Fingle Bridge and Hannicombe Wood

Fingle Bridge

Fields

Hore Wood

Hedge

Magnolia with snow in churchyard

Milk-churn cooler (17th century)

Orchard

Pathway near Cranbrook Castle

Piddledown Common

Prestonbury

River rock

River Teign

Shelter

Smoke and cloud

Trees on a hill

Spinsters Rock and Higher Shilstone Farm

Two Moors Way

Trees along the River Teign

Woodland – split rock

Woodland – Boulder

Bradmere Pool

Blackaller Quarry and Kiln village

Blackaller Quarry

In 1861 there were fifty people living at Blackaller, in the self-contained community of Kiln village. There was a wheel-wright, a blacksmith, a carpenter, a baker as well as the quarry-men. Some of their wives were serge weavers; the teazels still grow there between the last house to be occupied and the quarry pit.

There were three white lime seams in the grey limestone face of the pit. The lime was in great demand, not only to use on the land but also for mixing with mortar. The hard stone was used for building roads and walls. Copper, silver, lead, tin and gold were all discovered at Blackaller.

By 1906 only one of the seams was still being worked. Then one weekend the pump that kept the pit dry broke down. The pit was flooded and abandoned. In 1931 a reservoir was built on the hill above, filled with water pumped up from the pit and then piped to the village.

In 1960 there were still twenty-five men working at the quarry, by now making tarmac from the crushed stone. The quarry was finally closed 1991. Not much remains of the houses and the lime kilns, the water in the pit is now at least sixty feet deep covering the workmen's shed and tools, and the later buildings are derelict and overgrown.

Roger Chudley

Roger was born in the village in 1938 at Broad Meadow Cottage. He started work in Chagford as a plumber in 1953. He went on to do National Service after which he started work in the Devon Quarry in 1961. For the first five or six years he drove a loader (the quarry also had a contract for clearing the snow for Devon County Council) carrying limestone for making tarmac and walling (about 30 tons per hour produced by the tarmac plant).

Bardon Roadstone took over and put in a new tarmac plant, then they produced about 300 tons a day. The wages were never high and he worked long hours (5am to 5pm each day plus weekends). They did all the repairs to equipment themselves. Closing down came out of the blue not long after Bardon Roadstone took over, with only about three weeks' notice given in December 1991.

Roger Chudley – Foreman/weighbridge attendant

Jack Holter – excavator

Gordon Groydon – tarmac maker

Jack Pook – plant engineer

Mervyn Saffin – mechanic

John Easterbrook – stone crusher

Clarence Bridgeman – lorry driver

Jonathon Bint – crusher/driver

Wayne Mudge – loader/driver

129

Path leading to Kiln village

House chimney Kiln village

Quarry pit

Teazle

Quarry building

Lime kilns

Doorway to old Bakery

Window and chair

Work tools

Van

Toilets

137

Fuel tank

Swarfega

Beckmeter

Since these photos were taken there have been some changes in the parish:

Arthur Westcott, died at the age of 97 peacefully sitting in the garden. Georgina Robinson,
Norman Webber and Joan Gowing-Scopes have also died.

Some of the pets shown in the photos are also now dead – the dogs Coley,
Penny and Tappell and Fluffy the guinea pig.

New babies have been born, including Olivia Rubbra, Tilly Dixon, Oliver Loram,
Lucy Mudge, and Ellie, a sister for Jessie Guscott.

Exhibitions and Publications

Exhibitions:

Another York (group)	Derwent College, York University	1982
Photographs 1979 – 1982	Impressions Gallery, York	1982
	Fingerprints Gallery, London	1983
Brimham Rocks	Open Eye Gallery, Liverpool	1983
	Bicton Studio Gallery, Exmouth	1983
	Art Centre, York	1985
The 4th Brunel Photo Show (selected prints)	Brunel University	1983
Variations on a Moor (commissioned by Impressions, sponsored by Ilford)	Impressions Gallery, York (touring North Yorkshire)	1983 – 1984
Our City (group)	Art Centre, York	1986
Architecture/Formalism/ Photography (group)	Untitled Gallery, Sheffield	1986 – 1987
The 8th Brunel Photo Show (portfolio – Plumpton)	Brunel University	1987
With Walls & Towers Girdled (group)	Impressions Gallery, York	1988
River Fosse (group)	Impressions Gallery, York	1990
Various (group)	Beningborough Hall, Nth Yorkshire	1990

Mixed photographs	The Art Haven group, Exeter	1999
Rural Time, Drewsteignton	Castle Drogo, Devon	2001
Drewsteignton – A portrait of a Dartmoor Parish and its people (formerly known as Rural Time)	Museum of Dartmoor Life, Okehampton	2001
Drewsteignton – A portrait of a Dartmoor Parish and its people (formerly known as Rural Time)	1st Sight Gallery, (Wonford Hospital, Exeter)	2001

Publications:

Brimham Rocks	Amateur Photographer	1983
Variations on a Moor	Creative Camera	1983
Growing Space	Amateur Photographer	1987
Rural Time, Drewsteignton	What Digital Camera	2001
Drewsteignton – A portrait of a Dartmoor Parish and its people (formerly known as Rural Time)	Devon Life Magazine	2001

Planned Exhibition

Drewsteignton – A portrait of a Dartmoor Parish and its people (formerly known as Rural Time)	High Moorland Visitor Centre, Princetown, Devon	early 2002

Not completed or never shown:

Hackfall	1990 – 1991
Clifton Moor	1991
Nudes	1991